To Dr. Bradley
God Bless
Dr. M
:)

Preaching to Empty Seats

Over One Hundred Steps to Fill God's House with People, Power, and Praise

Dr. C. Dexter Wise III

WESTBOW PRESS®
A DIVISION OF THOMAS NELSON
& ZONDERVAN

Copyright © 2015 Dr. C. Dexter Wise III.

All rights reserved. No part of this book may be used or reproduced by any means, graphic, electronic, or mechanical, including photocopying, recording, taping or by any information storage retrieval system without the written permission of the publisher except in the case of brief quotations embodied in critical articles and reviews.

Scripture taken from the New King James Version. Copyright © 1979, 1980, 1982 by Thomas Nelson, Inc. Used by permission. All rights reserved.

Scripture taken from the King James Version of the Bible.

WestBow Press books may be ordered through booksellers or by contacting:

WestBow Press
A Division of Thomas Nelson & Zondervan
1663 Liberty Drive
Bloomington, IN 47403
www.westbowpress.com
1 (866) 928-1240

Because of the dynamic nature of the Internet, any web addresses or links contained in this book may have changed since publication and may no longer be valid. The views expressed in this work are solely those of the author and do not necessarily reflect the views of the publisher, and the publisher hereby disclaims any responsibility for them.

Any people depicted in stock imagery provided by Thinkstock are models, and such images are being used for illustrative purposes only. Certain stock imagery © Thinkstock.

ISBN: 978-1-5127-0575-1 (sc)
ISBN: 978-1-5127-0574-4 (hc)
ISBN: 978-1-5127-0573-7 (e)

Library of Congress Control Number: 2015912244

Print information available on the last page.

WestBow Press rev. date: 8/31/2015

Contents

The Lying Tree vii

Part I
Contributing Factors

Empty Preacher 3
Empty Preaching 9
Empty People 17
Empty Praise 23
Empty Plate 27
Empty Place 33
Empty Programs 37
Empty Promotion 41
Empty Plans 45

Part II
More than One Hundred Steps to Fill God's
House with People, Power, and Praise

The Preacher 53
The Preaching 57
The People 61
The Place 67
The Praise 73
The Plate 79
The Programs 81
The Promotion 87
The Plans 95

A Parting Prayer 97

The Lying Tree

Thanks to my legendary mother, Rev. Virginia Wise, and my late, great pastor, Dr. Montague J. Brackett, I was introduced to the Hampton Institute Ministers' Conference at an early age. As a result, I was blessed to literally sit at the feet of some of the best, brightest, and *baddest* preachers on the planet.

The first row in the Memorial Chapel, where the conference was held in my youth, was reserved for past presidents. So I came early each night and situated myself on the second row less than twenty feet from the podium. At ground zero, I listened to every word, soaked in every sentence, and never let any of those gospel giants' words fall to the ground.

Across the street, within a stone's throw of the chapel was a large shade tree. I was told that this tree was called "the lying tree." At first, I didn't know why they called it that, but I soon found out. For some reason or another, it was in the cool shade of this tree that preachers from all around the country were prone to or even compelled to lie.

To say that they exaggerated would be kind. They didn't exaggerate. They straight out lied. They lied about how big their annual budget was. They lied about the size of their salaries. They lied about the seating capacity of their sanctuary. They lied about the cars they drove (which were actually rented). They lied about the women they had on the side. They lied about how many revivals they had done that year. They lied about how many members they had. They lied about how many people they preached to every Sunday.

I shall never forget standing under that tree listening to a "big-time" preacher from New York hold court about his church. About ten of us stood mesmerized as he told us about his megaministry. He said he had ten thousand members and five thousand students in Sunday school every Sunday.

At sixteen years old, that blew me away. I couldn't imagine that many people going to one church every week. And to think of five thousand people in Sunday school when our church would have been excited to have fifty on Easter was absolutely beyond my comprehension. I left the tree that day picturing myself being the pastor of such an amazing and humungous church.

On my way from the tree to the cafeteria, another preacher who had also been with me beneath the tree pulled me to the side. He said, "Young man, I saw you over there. I just want to tell you not to believe all of that stuff. In the first place, his raggedy old church wouldn't even hold ten thousand people. And second, he's lucky if he sees one hundred people on Sunday."

What is it about us preachers that makes us lie about our ministry? We want to give the impression that we're doing so well. We want to make people think that everything is fine.

We want to let people know that we're in charge. And instead of telling the truth, we lie.

The truth is, the deacons are fighting us. The bank is hounding us. The building is falling in all around us. The members have abandoned us. Our wives are about to leave us. Our children are embarrassing us. Our colleagues are laughing at us.

The seeds of these lies sprout from the soil of low self-esteem. Negative peer pressure waters them until they become false expectations for ministry, and this causes preachers to be forced to live two lives—the life of the lies and the life of the miserable ministry we lead.

The inspiration for this book came during a rare moment of public pastoral transparency. I was invited to preach the tenth-anniversary service of a friend. In his remarks, after the sermon, he thanked me for encouraging him. He admitted that, honestly, there were many times during those ten years when he wanted to quit.

He continued to openly confess publicly how disappointed he was after ten years. His church had made many accomplishments with which others would have been elated. However, he liberally vented his frustration and asked out loud in the presence of his members and mine, "What do I have to do to make people come to church? I give my best. I sacrifice for them, and yet my church remains empty. I wish I knew what to do."

When he said that, I didn't just hear it—I felt it. In fact, tears came to my eyes because I knew the feeling. I knew what it was like to have prepared a delicious sermonic supper all week and then come to church on Sunday and have virtually nobody there to enjoy it. When he asked those questions, he was not talking directly to me, but I wanted to tell him, "I know what you can do about those empty seats." It was right then that the title and task of this book dropped into my spirit.

This book is what I burned to tell him and all the preachers like us who from time to time preach to empty seats. This work is an attempt on my part to examine those empty seats and provide practical steps on how to fill those empty seats.

In the first part of this book, I identify nine factors that contribute to empty seats. I discuss these factors in a descriptive way. That is, I describe what they are and how they generate empty seats in the church. These nine factors may be seen as a checklist to begin your search for the thieves that rob your Sunday-morning sanctuary of occupants.

The second part of this presentation is a list of more than one hundred steps that pastors and churches can take to fill those empty seats. Just one of these recommendations may not only fill your empty seats but also revolutionize your entire ministry.

It is my hope and prayer that, as a result of this book, your empty seats in the sanctuary will be filled and that countless lost souls will flood into the kingdom of God, full of the Word of God, full of the Spirit of God, and full of the power of God.

Part I

Contributing Factors

Empty Preacher

Whether you know it, believe it, or are willing to admit it, there is a connection between empty seats and an empty preacher. Sometimes there is so much chaos in the church that the connection is a blurred line. Oftentimes, due to the preacher's acts of omission, the connection is a dotted line. Frequently, as a result of the preacher's sins of commission, the connection is a straight line. Then, in rare but real instances, due to the preacher's past and personality, the connection is an equal sign. Nevertheless, there is a connection between empty seats and an empty preacher.

In a certain sense, it seems quite unfair to place the responsibility for empty seats at the feet of the preacher. What about offensive church officers who refuse to change? What about apathetic members who couldn't care less? What about an increasingly secular society that has less and less tolerance and time for the church? What about a poor economy that forces would-be churchgoers to work on Sundays? Surely the preacher is not singly and fully to blame for all of those empty seats. True enough.

However, what was true for President Harry Truman in the White House is just as true for the preacher in the church house. In spite of all the hands that touch it, all the eyes that see it, and all the ones that pass it, the buck stops at the preacher's feet. Furthermore, the explanation of so many empty seats rightly starts there—for an empty preacher can very easily and quickly empty the seats.

Make no mistake about it: there is a difference between a full preacher and an empty preacher. For the full preacher, Sunday can't get there fast enough. For the empty preacher, Sunday comes far too soon. For the full preacher, the pulpit is a mountaintop from which to proclaim, "Thus saith the Lord!" For the empty preacher, the pulpit is merely a stage from which to recite rehearsed lines. For the full preacher, prophetic words spout out as righteous indignation. For the empty preacher, piercing words spew forth as unbridled rage.

For the full preacher, the sermon overflows with grace. For the empty preacher, the message devolves into a tirade of gripes. For the full preacher, the parishioners are seen as a flock of hungry sheep, dying to be fed. For the empty preacher, the parishioners are regarded as a pack of ravenous wolves that have gathered to watch the preacher die.

An empty preacher feeds others but does so with frustration. An empty preacher faithfully delivers the gospel but has a hard time being fresh. An empty preacher can be counted on to show up but is more burned out than filled up. An empty preacher hears the command of Jesus, "If you love Me, feed my sheep," but is so preoccupied with his or her own starvation that he or she hardly has time or energy to nourish others. An empty preacher may have once sought success but now would be satisfied with mere survival.

This difference is discernible by those who occupy the sanctuary seats. They feel it. They are affected by it. They are hurt by it. They talk about it. They complain about it. They are turned off by it.

They assemble at church expecting victory, but instead they get venom. They journey to the house of God to hear about justice, but instead they are served judgment. They rush to the service seeking salvation, but instead they find cynicism. They come for confirmation, but instead they receive condemnation. They leave their respective places looking for true love, but instead they are given a tongue-lashing. Over time, rather than subject themselves to such treatment from the pulpit, they vacate the premises and thus leave empty seats.

What happened? How does this happen to preachers? Of course, there may be as many reasons for this as there are empty preachers. However, the following are among the reasons why preachers become or are empty.

First, some are empty because they were never full in the first place. Paul ran into such well-meaning disciples in Ephesus and asked them, "'Have ye received the Holy Ghost since you believed?' And they said unto him, 'We have not so much as heard whether there be any Holy Ghost'" (Acts 19:1–2). Imagine that! They were followers, disciples, and leaders, and yet they had never heard of the Holy Ghost. Needless to say, if they had never heard of it, they had never been filled with it.

It is an unfortunate fact that not everyone who fills the pulpit has been filled with the Holy Ghost. Therefore, they preach on their own power. They minister by mimicking others. They talk and teach with natural talents instead of speaking based on a spiritual gifting and anointing. No matter how talented they may be, their human power will soon run out, and they will find themselves empty.

Second, some are empty because they were once full and somehow developed a slow leak. At the first sound of their call, they regularly rushed to the throne of God to receive their daily dosage of revelation. In the beginning, there was a fire burning in their bones. When they first started in the ministry, they sought to save the whole world. But over time, little by little, incident by incident, tiny holes punctured the inner linings of their souls, and slow leaks developed.

Trusted friends disappointed them, and they lost faith in people. They were hit by brutal body blows in board meetings, and they lost confidence in themselves. They sustained public punches to the face in church meetings, and they lost respect in the eyes of their own congregation. Their recommendations to advance the ministry were routinely rejected, and they lost the desire to make a difference. Their tireless efforts were unrecognized and unrewarded, and they lost their willingness to sacrifice. Their sermons fell on deaf ears, and they lost their commitment to preparation.

After a series of sustained slow leaks, these empty preachers develop an attitude that says, "If they don't care, why should I?" At this point, there may still be heat in the preacher, but there is no fire. There may still be light in the preacher, but there is no lightning. There may still be information coming from the preacher, but there is no revelation. The air is gone. The message is flat. The vessel is dry because over time, what once filled the preacher has leaked out and has never been replaced.

Third, some are empty because they had a major blowout. In contrast to the empty preachers who experienced a slow leak, they became empty because of a sudden blowout. They were riding merrily along in ministry, surfing on waves of spiritual success, and serving with enviable effectiveness. Then suddenly, out of the blue, an explosion took place.

When a blowout happens, the preacher loses control. When a blowout takes place, even though they are not driving, the safety and lives of those who travel and keep company with the preacher are in danger. When a blowout occurs, innocent bystanders and vehicles in the proximity can also get hit. Therefore, while the blowout may empty the preacher, it can also literally take the lives of others.

Many are the preachers who have had blowouts and thus been blown out of effectiveness in ministry. Personal indiscretions have blown out their credibility. Catastrophic financial losses have blown out their security. A messy marital breakup has blown out their image. Church splits have blown out their love for God's people. Health issues have blown out their faith. False accusations have blown out their reputation. Wayward children have blown out their hearts. All at once, in the twinkling of an eye, a preacher who was sailing high is now sinking and empty because of a blowout.

Fourth and finally, some are empty because they are like hoses that allowed water to pass through but never saved any water for themselves. The water that passed through them was living water. It was refreshing water. It was divine water. It was healing water. However, in their sincere and urgent desire to deliver pure water to others, these preachers never made any provisions to keep some of that water for themselves.

Hence, they continued to thirst as they refreshed others. They remained hungry as they fed others. They were discouraged as they encouraged others. They were lost as they saved others. Because of the water that passed through the preacher, the people prospered. However, since the preacher poured it all out, he or she had none left to live on. This leaves these preachers empty.

Thankfully, an empty preacher is not always a sign of suffering. More often than not, a preacher's emptiness is a sign of service. That is to say, the reason a preacher is empty is because he or she has spent his or her spiritual fuel in service. The reason we keep going back to the gas station is because we have used our fuel in traveling. The gas tanks of parked and garaged cars never become empty.

In this case, the empty preacher is not to be pitied but praised. The solution to this is simple: go back to the Holy Ghost gas station, open your tank, and fill it up. The gas was already paid for at Calvary. Therefore, there is no need to remain empty, for "[t]here is a fountain filled with blood / drawn from Immanuel's veins / and sinners plunge beneath that flood / lose all their guilt and stain."

Empty Preaching

What if the problem is not the preacher? Suppose instead the culprit for the empty seats is the preaching. Many are the preachers who have directly or indirectly heard the following speech in so many words: "Pastor, you know I love you. I will always love you and First Lady. You dedicated me as a baby. You baptized me as a child. You married me and my husband as young adults. You preached Momma's funeral. You are a great man of God. But I have to leave you because I am not being fed." What they are suggesting is that the problem is not the preacher as a person. It is the person as a preacher.

A preacher or pastor could be full of integrity, a model of stability, a paradigm of responsibility, and a perfect example of charity. However, this same preacher could create empty seats because his or her preaching is not filling the people in the seats. These people feel empty when they leave, and therefore, they go elsewhere.

One of the most frustrating realities in ministry is that many preachers with virtually no integrity and even less morality preach to a packed house every Sunday. Then those who are humble, faithful, and Christ like are forced to preach to empty seats. The fact is, many churchgoers are willing and able to overlook the faults of an imperfect preacher if what the preacher is preaching continues to feed and fill them.

This fact is no license for faithful preachers to go out and act the fool just to fill their empty seats! Rather, it is a wakeup call for all preachers to revisit and reexamine their preaching to see what it must be in order to fill and feed their hearers. All of this is so that the faithful will, in turn, continue to fill the seats.

Here are seven reasons why sermons tend to seem empty.

1. Empty sermons are not well prepared.

Sermons are prepared in many ways. They are prepared in the preacher's private prayer time alone and listening to God. They are prepared through reading and researching texts in concordances and commentaries. They are prepared upon the foundation of formal or informal training. They are prepared by assembling nuggets throughout the week. They are prepared with a lifetime of experiences.

The length of preparation is not always the critical issue. Some of the best sermons come from God virtually prepackaged and "pre-pared." The type of preparation does not have to be standard. What works for one preacher may not work for another. However, some preparation is required, and when it is not there, it shows.

To be sure, great preachers are able to preach off the cuff and slay those who hear them. (I must confess that some of my best sermons have been four o'clock specials that came to me in the car on the way to an afternoon service.) Yet, it should be remembered that this off-the-cuff preaching comes from the overflow of a reservoir built up after years of preaching and preparing to preach. Preaching without preparation should be the exception, not the rule.

There used to be a time when the preacher was the only one who knew what a concordance was, not to mention owned one or knew how to use it. Now all the people in the audience with a cell phone have a whole library of Bibles, commentaries, and dictionaries at their fingertips to fact check as they listen.

There used to be a time when the preacher was the most educated person in the room. Today, even little children are better educated on certain subjects than the preacher will ever be. The bottom line is that today's congregation is made up of far better prepared people than ever before. They deserve a prepared message and can easily detect one that is not.

A preacher who faithfully stands on the wall and proclaims the gospel on a regular basis will be given a pass for a flunk or a mediocre message every now and then. But a consistent lack of preparation that leads to a history and expectation of weak sermons is inexcusable. People then decide to excuse themselves from the inexcusable and leave empty seats.

2. Empty sermons are not pointed.

Sermons are not just about people. They are for people and to people. As such, sermons can very easily fall flat when they are not suited for the people to whom they are being delivered. It is entirely possible, therefore, that on its own, a sermon is an excellent sermon, but if it is preached to the wrong crowd, what may have been excellent can become awful.

Great and effective sermons are aimed at and meet the needs of the people who hear them. They are in their language. They are on their level. They are in their range of experience. They are addressing their needs. They are healing their hurts. They are answering their questions.

Preachers do not get extra brownie points for preaching to and trying to impress those who are not even in the room. One of the greatest mistakes preachers can make is to preach to and about those who should be or could be in the empty seats while failing to minister to the ones filling the seats, sitting right there in front of them.

Here is how it works. If you preach about and rail on the people who should be in the empty seats, you annoy and take time away from those who made an effort to come. Doing too much of this causes you to risk losing the ones who are there, thus creating more empty seats.

However, if you preach to the ones who are there, as if the church is packed wall to wall, the present ones will be inspired and motivated to bring others with them the next time to fill the empty seats beside them. Yes, be aware of the empty seats. You may even acknowledge the empty seats, but when you preach focus on the ones in the full seats.

3. Empty sermons are not well presented.

Have you ever had a teacher who clearly knew her stuff but was a terrible teacher? Have you ever heard a preacher with more degrees than a thermometer but couldn't preach his way out of a wet paper bag? Of course you have.

In these cases, it is obvious that preachers are perfectly prepared and quite qualified. No one disputes that they have command of the information. Their problem is not that they lack command of the information. Rather, it is that they are unable to clearly and effectively communicate that information.

They ramble. They go off on tangents. They give too much information. They strain at gnats. They talk over your head. They can't be followed because what they are saying doesn't follow. They use big words that they don't explain. They are brilliant, but you don't get it because of the way it is being presented.

This is one reason why Jesus received such a great response as the people heard Him gladly. He spoke in parables and with authority, not like the Scribes and Pharisees. Part of the preparation and pointing of a sermon involves giving some consideration to how to present it. This should be done in such a manner that the hearers not only get it but also can run with it.

4. Empty sermons are not preached with purpose.

Preaching was not intended to be an exercise for a minister's vocal chords. Each sermon should have a purpose. During preparation, the preacher would do well to ask, "What is the aim of this sermon? What is the purpose of preaching on this subject to this group at this time?" Failing to self-consciously ask such purpose questions can lead to weak preaching, which usually fails the "so-what test."

You listen to a sermon for thirty minutes to an hour. You watch the preacher perspire with handkerchief in hand. Then, when it's all over, if you can't answer the question: "So what?" the sermon has been unsuccessful. "So what was the preacher really saying? So what does that text teach me about my situation? So what does that have to do with me? So what should make me care?"

Preaching done with a purpose anticipates each of these so-what questions and answers them throughout the sermon. Strong sermons, therefore, are not only preached on purpose, but they are also preached with a purpose.

5. Empty sermons are not practical.

Closely connected with a lack of purpose is the tendency that empty sermons are not practical. They can be rhetorical and full of flowery language. They can be theological and overloaded with heavy German and Latin phrases. They can be philosophical, raising timeless questions. They can even be comical, with anecdotes and jokes galore.

Nevertheless, at the end of the day, sermon hearers ask: "What do you want me to do with this, and how do I do it? You just told me what God said I should do, but how do I do it? You just showed me what a godly marriage should be like, but how do I make my marriage like that?"

Preachers do their parishioners a disservice when they only preach the what and the why but not the how. For the most part, people who come to church on a regular basis already know the what and the why. Their challenge is the how. They already know the Ten Commandments, but they don't know how to avoid worshiping other gods. They already know the Lord's Prayer, but they don't know how to forgive those who trespass against them. They already know that God will supply all of their need according to His riches in glory, but they don't know how to act until He does.

Throughout the course of a year, there undoubtedly will be many sermons delivered as straight proclamation (i.e., Thus saith the Lord! Period.). Still, for the most part, even when people hear proclamation, they are also eager for the preacher to add some practical application.

6. Empty sermons are not powerful.

Preaching can be pretty but not powerful. Preaching can be polished but not powerful. Preaching can be well organized but not powerful. Preaching can be logical but not powerful. Preaching can be creative but not powerful.

Powerful preaching has the ability to penetrate our facades and touch our hearts. Powerful preaching changes minds and lives. Powerful preaching restores families and wrecked relationships. Powerful preaching causes people to run crying, "What must I do to be saved?"

Powerful preaching is the result of being connected to the power behind preaching, then getting out of the way and letting that power do its work. A nice sermon comes off as a great speech. However, a great sermon is felt as the powerful life-changing word of the living God for me today!

7. Empty sermons are not portable.

The easiest way to get the sermon to the masses that might have been in the empty seats is to hand it over to the ones who were actually present. Yet this is a challenge for so many churchgoers because when asked by those who were absent, "What did the preacher preach about?" they say, "I don't know, but it sure was good!"

Well, I beg to differ. It wasn't good unless it was portable—that is, presented or preserved in such a way that at least some parts of it could be recited and repeated by one who heard it to one who did not. No one expects the congregation to be able to remember every word. The preacher can't even do that. Still, the sermon should be titled, designed, structured, and delivered in such a way that even a little child can carry some of it home and share it with his or her friends.

Many of the issues involving how and what to preach are addressed in my book *Everything You Need to Preach Like a Pro!* Please allow me to refer you to it to find loads of concrete suggestions on how to do what I have argued here that preachers must do when they preach.

Empty People

Our investigation into the source of the empty seats in the sanctuary began with the preacher and that preacher's preaching. The impact and import of these two factors alone can never be overstated. However, common sense and personal experience will confirm that while our investigation may start there, the preacher and the preaching cannot possibly be the whole story.

In fact, those on the other side of the podium cannot escape without owning some of the responsibility for the empty seats. The preacher is connected to the empty seats, but so are the people. What we are acknowledging here is not so much that the people of the church are themselves empty. Rather, it is that their actions, reactions, and inactions can and do play a pivotal part in emptying the seats of the church.

More than thirty years ago, when I first arrived as the twenty-seven-year-old pastor of an historic Midwest church, I was the new kid on the block. I was received with great fanfare from the governor of the state to the mayor of the city and all across the board. Our whole church was excited about the possibilities of what God could do with us together.

Soon after my coming, people began to regularly join the church by the dozens. Every Sunday, hundreds packed the church, and new members streamed down the aisle. In time, though, I noticed something quite puzzling. While new members were steadily joining the church, they were soon gone.

At first I assumed it was because we needed to do a better job assimilating them into the church. Then I thought they might have been caught up in the moment after a rousing message and only joined the church as an impulsive reaction. I am embarrassed to confess that it took me years to find out what the real problem was. I didn't discover the reason on purpose. It was revealed to me when I providentially ran into one of those ex-new members in a restaurant.

When I inquired about her whereabouts, she proceeded to tell me the reason she joined the church was because of my preaching. It blessed her. It challenged her. It inspired her. It changed her. However, the reason she stopped coming was because of the people.

She indicated that they made her feel so bad simply because she was new. They constantly reminded her that she had just gotten there. They protected certain seats. They protested every positive step the pastor proposed to take the church forward. In so many words, she said, "There are a lot of good people at your church, but I didn't come to fight, so I left. Now I watch you on TV at home without having to bother with all of that!"

A man who was six foot eight and weighed more than three hundred pounds joined our church. I actually baptized him. Given his size, I suggested that he join our newly created security ministry, which he gladly did. He was stationed at one of the front doors, and after a few short weeks, he too disappeared. When I finally caught up with him, he told me that he was not only leaving the security ministry but the church as well.

Apparently he had been standing at the door and a senior member of the church told him that our church did not need any security, and as she walked by him, she whacked him with her cane! Now, this man could have picked her up and put her in his pocket with one finger, but the thought that an old lady would strike him in the church was too much for him to bear.

I have many more stories of how members have been responsible for others not coming back to the church or not coming to the church at all. More than likely, you do too. As quiet as it is kept, long before guests ever hear the pastor, they meet the members. The way they are treated by those members often becomes the deciding factor in whether they stay for the rest of the service or ever come back at all.

Grouchy greeters, unfriendly ushers, cold congregants, and overzealous security are all straws on the camel's back. At some point, no matter how good the preacher or the sermon is, the camel's back is broken, and as a result, there are more empty seats.

Here are some common ways the people of the church can contribute to the number of empty seats.

- They create empty seats by not giving literal or figurative space to guests and new members.
- They create empty seats by opening the doors of the church on Sunday but closing opportunities for

membership and leadership in ministry the rest of the week.
- They create empty seats by protecting their own seats and using their coats to cover the empty seats beside them.
- They create empty seats by projecting an attitude of complacency, suggesting that the status quo is just fine.
- They create empty seats with snide and sarcastic remarks about people's dress and appearance.
- They create empty seats by blocking the very plans and programs that will advance the kingdom of Christ, win souls, and fill the empty seats.
- They create empty seats by missing the chance to minister to members at the very moments of crisis when they need it most.
- They create empty seats by not noticing that the person who used to sit in that empty seat is no longer there.
- They create empty seats when they forget what they were like before they were saved.
- They create empty seats when they consider an empty seat as an opportunity to stretch out instead of motivation to reach out.
- They create empty seats when they speak ill of their church and pastor in the community.
- They create empty seats when they pass the total responsibility to fill those seats on to the pastor.
- They create empty seats when their work at the church occurs during the worship hour and therefore, causes

them to be absent during the worship. (e.g., trustees counting money, volunteers in the nursery, or security members roaming the building and grounds.)
- They create empty seats when their entire ministry is confined to their own facility.
- They create empty seats when they see the church as a refuge from the world instead of a resource to the world.
- They create empty seats when they have no programs for children and youth who will grow up and eventually fill their seats.

When I hear of the small things that cause individuals to leave the church, I get angry with the people for leaving over such a small thing. Then at the same time, I get angry with the seasoned church members because they should have known better than to do what they did to drive others away. Empty seats are not all the preacher's fault!

Empty Praise

Empty praise means empty presence. Empty presence leads to empty seats. Remember how the Psalmist referred to God: "But thou art holy, O thou that inhabitest the praises of Israel" (Psalm 22:3 KJV). The presence of God is not causally or coincidentally found in the praise of God's people, Israel. His presence inhabits or lives in those praises. The New King James version of this same verse makes it even clearer by saying that God is enthroned in the praises of Israel. Thus, God lives in and reigns in His praise.

Consequently, the best, quickest, and easiest way to drum up the presence of God is to praise God. When we praise Him, He shows up. When He shows up, people show up to worship, adore, and experience Him. The regular, predictable presence of God in the church creates an anticipation and expectation on the part of the people that it is there that they can meet God.

Of course, God is everywhere and can be praised anywhere. However, the concentrated congregational praise that routinely takes place in His house makes that place different than any other building. It's the presence that draws the people and the praise that draws the presence.

Therefore, when the praises of the Lord die out, die down, or completely disappear, then so does His felt presence. When this happens, those who frequent that church have no expectation that their experience in worship will be any different than going to the meat market.

Thousands of beautiful buildings are relatively empty because they have stiff worship. This worship does not allow the congregation to freely praise the Lord and therefore does not give time or space for the presence of the Lord to flow. The worship is on a timer. The order of worship has already been carved in stone in the bulletin. The hymns only have so many verses. If the Lord does not appear within these parameters, then too bad. Maybe He will show up next week.

Many also are those who attend churches where the praise and worship is stuck. It has been the same for decades. Same sad songs. Same old robes. Same dusty books. Same worn-out instruments. Same tired people. There is nothing new, nothing fresh, and nothing exciting. When guests enter these churches, it's like they stepped out of their own time into some other earlier time zone.

For still others, the praise and worship at their church is stale. It's there, but it does not bring Him there. It happens on cue, but it has no hallelujah. It can be heard, but it cannot be felt. It's played live, but it has lost its luster. Nobody buys stale bread beyond its expiration date. The same goes for stale worship.

To ensure that worship does not start or become stiff, stuck, or stale, the Psalmist suggests the following:

> Make a joyful shout to the Lord, all you lands! Serve the Lord with gladness; Come before His presence with singing. Know that the Lord, He is God; It is He who has made us, and not we ourselves; We are His people and the sheep of His pasture. Enter into His gates with thanksgiving, And into His courts with praise. (Psalm 100:1–4)

Praise is so powerful because of these qualities:

- Praise is like Lysol; it disinfects the room of demonic spirits and depressing thoughts.
- Praise is like perfume; it fills the sanctuary with a sweet aroma.
- Praise is like good music; it changes the mood and creates an atmosphere for worship.
- Praise takes the focus off of people and their problems and puts the focus where it belongs—on God.
- Praise turns worship from solemn to celebration.
- Praise sets the stage for miracles.

There are thousands of churches that offer a stiff, stuck, and stale worship experience. There are many who enjoy and appreciate it. However, for the most part, churches that only offer this are not growing and are full of empty seats.

In the growing churches, no matter the denomination, praise is not just a warm up to worship. It is given prime time in worship. Praise is not segregated or separated from the worship. Praise saturates every aspect of the worship. Praise is not restricted to songs but comes forth in dance, mime, step, flags, sign language, and many other forms of gospel arts. Praise may be led by a praise team, but it soon involves and envelops the whole congregation.

You may not be able to immediately fill the empty seats with people, but you can fill the empty sanctuary with praise. When you fill the sanctuary with praise, it will draw the people to fill the seats.

> "And I, if I be lifted up from the earth, will draw all men unto me" (John 12:32).

Empty Plate

Empty pockets create empty plates, and empty plates lead to empty seats. It is hard to tell which of these is most critical or which of these comes first. However, there is no doubt that when the parishioners' pockets are empty, then the church's offering plate will be relatively empty. When the church's plate is empty, so will be its ability to do ministry and thus, the number of people it can serve.

It's really not that deep. It takes money to do ministry. The love we offer is free. The service we give is free. The teaching we provide is free. The joy we share is free. The salvation we preach is free. But while each of these may themselves be free, the delivery of them in an institutional setting is not free.

The staff that offers these services is not free. The church building in which this staff works has a mortgage and maintenance costs that are not free. The supplies and equipment for the ministry are not free. The list could easily go on and on. The harsh reality is that while salvation is free, establishing, maintaining, developing, and expanding churches is not free.

Let's begin with the empty pockets. Lack of income, unemployed members, hurricanes, floods, and an overall economic downturn are all factors over which the church has no control. The church does not control the stock market. The church does not make political and economic policy. The church does not create natural disasters. The church does not force outdated factories out of business.

Yet, while the church has no control over any of these, all of them affect the amount of income its members have to give to the church. If the members don't get it, they can't give it.

Now, when the members don't have money to regularly give in the offering plate, at least two things happen. One, they stop coming to church altogether because they feel embarrassed that they can no longer contribute or contribute at the level they used to. Church is a place to give. Right or wrong, some ask, "If I can't give, why go?"

A second thing that can happen when the members don't have money is that now, the church itself can't give. It no longer has the resources to offer the ministry it used to or desires to. It has to cut back and cut out. It is forced to give more priority to literally keeping the church doors open than "opening the doors of the church." It becomes more concerned with keeping the lights on than being the light of the world.

The pressure caused by the empty plate causes each worship service to be filled with more and more pleas for finances than for praise of the Lord. Eventually those looking for ministry get discouraged because it is not forthcoming. They then go to the big church down the street that seems to have its stuff together and have it all going on.

Other members who come to church looking for a refuge from the financial crisis at home get disgusted and turned off by the constant cries for money at church. They too are tempted to go to the big church down the street where it looks like all the bills are paid. Either way—empty seats.

Believers who leave you soon discover that the megachurches are really not doing that much better. It takes money to do ministry, but it takes mega money to do megaministry. The pitch may be a little more polished in the big church down the street, but the end product is the same. "We need more money to provide you the ministry you expect." Make no mistake about it. Many megachurches also have loads of empty seats.

So what can pastors and churches do about these empty plates that lead to empty seats? Here are a few suggestions.

1. Pray about it.

It may sound corny, but prayer changes things. Praying about the finances of the church shifts the emphasis from the people to God. That is to say, as I heard Dr. Jerome Barber of Hampton, Virginia, says: "I am a resource, but God is the Source."

Praying about the empty plates ultimately challenges people to look to God and not to themselves. God has resources we do not. God can open doors we cannot. Thus, in both private and public settings, people with faith can exercise their faith and call on a God who never fails.

2. Preach about it.

Sometimes the plate is empty because the people's pockets are truly empty, and they do not have it to give. Still, there are other times when the people have plenty of money, and they refuse to give it. Why they refuse to give could be the subject of another book. Suffice it to say that many of them have not been taught or challenged to grow in this area of their Christian walk.

Preaching and teaching a series on stewardship, which includes but is not limited to tithing, may make a difference. A word of caution: any such preaching or teaching should come from the angle of growing in our ability to trust God and our desire to be obedient to God. Preaching about tithing with a tone of desperation builds pressure and may even raise a few dollars, but it does not build faith.

3. Practice it.

Good stewardship must be practiced before it is preached. That is to say, the pastor and leaders of the church must be willing to do their part before they can demand it of the rest of the church. When those at the top practice good stewardship, it becomes an example to the rest of the church and a credible testimony to those who have not yet tried it.

4. Praise it.

Giving is what Christians should do, and therefore, they should not expect any special consideration for doing what they are supposed to do. Nevertheless, because many people don't do what they are supposed to do, it helps when those who do are encouraged and thanked. For example, this can be done and should be done without making those who do not tithe feel badly while thanking those who do. The point is to praise the ones who do and inspire the ones who could but don't.

5. Produce it.

In some cases, even if every member were a tither, it would still not be enough. Beyond bake sales, chicken dinners, and fish fries, nowadays, with such vehicles as community development corporations, churches are finding ways to create other significant streams of income to offset and subsidize ministry costs not covered by the plate. This includes such endeavors as: building rental, grants, day care centers, charter schools, farms, restaurants, transportation, housing, and more.

Empty Place

The old saying is, "You should never judge a book by its cover." But the fact is, we all do it all the time. In this age of microwaves, texts, tweets, and Instagram, we don't have time to read the whole book. We size up people, places, and things by their cover.

In the church arena, the cover by which we are judged is our church building or the place in which we worship. It is not always the case, but it is probably safe to say that in most instances, potential visitors and members see our place on the outside long before they ever get to interact with our people on the inside. The place, therefore, becomes their first impression of your church. If that first impression is not positively received or mitigated, it may well be their last and only impression.

As you evaluate your place in terms of its impact on empty seats, you may want to acknowledge the following "place" factors.

1. Location

What's true for real estate is also true for religion. Location! Location! Location! It does make a difference where your church is located. Every, and virtually any, geographical barrier can be overcome. However, it is much easier to fill empty seats if people do not have to find them in an out of the way place.

Is your church in a growing area or a declining area? Do the worshipers at your church worry about their cars while they are worshiping, or do they feel safe both inside and outside of your building? Is your church easy to find, or do first-time guests need Google Earth and an escort to get there on Sunday? Is it on a bus line, or is it way out in the woods? Are there compatible businesses, services, etc., near the church, or will members have to walk past nightclubs and loiterers just to get in the door?

Thousands of great churches have become ghost towns because what was once a great location no longer is. On the other hand, plenty of pioneering pastors have launched major ministries because, like *Star Trek*, they dared to go where no man had ever gone before. There they found a crowd waiting for them and eager to welcome them.

2. Attraction

Let's assume that your church building has a great location; if it is not attractive, it still becomes a drive-by church! What is it about the church building that makes it stand out and draws people to it? Are its grounds well kept? Does it have a sign giving usable information, or do readers have to guess what kind of church it is and when it meets?

Can those passing by see inside the church, or do stained glass and thick wooden doors make it look like it is the home of a secret society? Is its architecture interesting, or does it look like a great big unimaginative box? Is the exterior well kept, or are the shingles on the roof missing, the paint on the walls peeling, and the windows on the side boarded up?

The appearance of your church facility is your physical calling card. If it looks a mess, don't be surprised if no one ever returns your call!

3. Condition

Even in the roughest and most run-down neighborhoods, there is always at least one house that is in good condition. It may be surrounded by boarded-up vacant houses. It may be next door to a crack house, but you can tell that whoever lives in that house actually has some pride and cares. The grass is cut. The hedges are trimmed. There are flowers on the porch. The paint on the house is fresh. The backyard is neat.

The point is, even if you are in a less-than-desirable neighborhood, or even if where you are worshiping does not have the latest design, you can still maintain what you have and keep it in good working order. This will make you stand out all the more. Thus, it is not only the location or attraction of your church building but also its condition that matters.

4. Function

Churches built in the 1950s may be solid and even well maintained. However, they may not have been designed to be used the way ministry is done today. That is, certain rooms and areas may have to be redesigned and repurposed to match the ministry of today. For example, "Where will you place the big screen in the sanctuary between the pillars and the organ pipes?"

Some churches only have a place to worship and therefore, have to ask where other functions, such as classes and fellowship, will be addressed. It can be done and it must be done so your building is not just pretty but functional.

Is it cool in the summer and warm in the winter? Can you see from anywhere you sit? Can you hear what is going on? Can you find your way around? Are there enough restrooms? Are there steps that have to be negotiated?

It is not enough for the mechanical systems in the church to function properly. The building itself must function in such a way that the ministry systems also function well in it.

5. Emotion

Just as important as how the church building looks is how people feel when they look at it and spend time in it. Does it look like a holy house or a haunted house? It is more like a mall or a mausoleum? Does it feel like a home where you can relax or a museum where you had "better not touch *nothing*"? Do children love to come there, or do they say they can't wait to get out of there?

To change the mood in a building may only take a new color of paint or more lighting. Only remember: how people feel about what is going on in the church can be affected by how they feel when they are in the church.

Empty Programs

In general, people go to church because they love Jesus. However, they come to your church because they love the specific way you worship and serve Jesus. With hundreds of church options in any given metropolitan area, you must provide at least one strong reason why church seekers choose your church over the others. Otherwise, they will drive past your church and leave you with a bunch of empty seats.

It is therefore critical that a church, whose aim it is to grow, gives prayerful consideration to the programs or ministries it intends to offer to the public. These programs or ministries constitute the reasons why your church becomes a viable church choice.

Some of the reasons that compel the public to visit and join your church are chosen for you. You may just happen to be within walking distance of potential members. Hence, you are close enough for thrifty people to save on gas and near enough for them to be comfortable sending their children unaccompanied to church. You may turn out to be the only AME church in the city. This might be a sufficient cause for some dyed-in-the-wool AMEs who just moved into the city to seek you out. These are examples of advantages that you did not particularly create. However, to fill your empty seats, you must recognize and capitalize on them.

Other reasons that trigger people to choose your church over other churches may be the services you provide to them as members and guests. The list of these could be quite long and includes: a nursery during worship, a viable children's ministry, a credit union, fitness programs, counseling, and transportation.

Believe it or not, there is a crowd that chooses a church based on the opportunities it offers for them to serve. Not everyone comes to church to be served. Some come with their sleeves rolled up and ready to go to work. If your church only has room for choir members and ushers, then those who cannot sing or stand will have nothing to do besides sit. It is therefore incumbent upon churches that want to fill their empty seats to offer a variety of ways that people can fulfill their callings by serving in and through the church.

At our church, Faith Ministries, we require everyone who becomes a member to publicly state the ministry they will join at the time they are officially commissioned as members of the church. We have more than seventy-five ministries in which people can serve.

Our policy is that if none of these seventy-five is what they feel called to do, they can simply write a one-page proposal and submit it to me, the pastor. If it is reasonable and they are really serious, a plan is designed to develop and launch it. Without a bunch of red tape and time, it will soon be added to the list of our ministries. This allows us to keep members because they have a stake in the church and reach other current and prospective members who may have had the same interest but never had this option for service.

There are yet more who might select your church, not so much because of what you offer but the way you offer it. Every church has preaching and music, but not like yours. They come to you because of the way your preaching and music minister to them. Some will drive for miles past dozens of churches to get to you just for this.

It is sad but true. There are also those who opt for your church for reasons that have nothing to do with theology. They will attend your church because of the conveniences it offers. That would be features like: a great facility, ample parking, convenient worship times, nursery during worship, easy and safe location, a bookstore, or a coffee shop.

Many churches with mediocre preaching and music thrive because they offer outstanding conveniences. Look at it this way. Your local buffet may not offer gourmet cooking, but the choice of food is so great and the price is so low that hungry hordes flock there and always leave full.

Here again, the Master is our model. Jesus offered more than one ministry to those who followed Him. Matthew 9:35 lays out in plain view what His ministry program was and why He seldom preached to empty seats:

> Then Jesus went about all the cities and villages, teaching in their synagogues, preaching the

gospel of the kingdom, and healing every sickness and every disease among the people.

Careful consideration of this single verse will give us a strategy for ministry.

- **His ministry was not limited to one location.** Jesus went about all the cities and villages.
- **He had a teaching ministry.** This aimed at the minds and helped in the spiritual maturity of His disciples.
- **He had a preaching ministry.** This gospel that He preached touched hearts and saved souls.
- **He had a healing ministry.** With this, He addressed the real and felt needs of the crowd with healing for all manner of sicknesses and diseases. That includes those associated with mind, body, and soul.

Thus Jesus gave both the curious, the critical, and the committed many reasons to come, and that's why many came.

Here is the conclusion of the matter. The more reasons you give people to come to your church, the greater will be the number of people who actually come. As a pastor or church leader, you cannot focus only on the things that interest you. In order to fill your empty seats, you must offer multiple quality ministries and services that interest and are important to the people you are trying to attract.

Empty Promotion

Years ago, I asked a prominent businesswoman, "What is the secret to your success?" And almost as if she had been waiting for me to ask, she replied, "Early to bed. Early to rise. Work like the Devil and advertise!" Far be it from me to ever suggest that church folk should "work like the Devil." Still, this woman did have a point when she included the word *advertise*.

Maybe we feel that Christianity requires modesty. Perhaps it is because we have been drilled that Christianity necessitates humility. Or it's just that we are inclined to do what we do in secrecy. Whatever the reason behind it, when we fail to advertise, no one knows who we are, where we are, what we have, what we do, or how we can help them.

Many churches today do not have empty promotion. They are empty of promotion. That is, they have no conscious, thought-out strategy to promote their ministry. Thus, empty seats.

This has not always been so. Jesus seldom had a problem with empty seats. He could hardly go anywhere without a crowd gathering almost immediately. Before the age of network TV, cable TV, radio, Facebook, Twitter, and YouTube, Jesus could pack a house in no time flat. How did He do that so well and so fast?

The master marketer, Jesus, took advantage of and applied the following techniques:

1. The example of a changed life.

There is no better advertisement of a product, program, or person than to be confronted with an example of an individual whose life has been radically changed. Everywhere He went Jesus left a trail of such examples. Lazarus was raised from the dead. The blind man came seeing into the temple. The woman with the issue of blood went home cleansed. The lepers showed themselves to the priests.

Each of these and more had no need to give a major verbal testimony. The change that Jesus wrought in their lives spoke for itself. Because of them, others wanted to meet and spend time with Him.

2. The recommendation of satisfied customers.

It is said that word of mouth is the number one and most effective means of advertisement. Even when Jesus specifically asked people not to tell anyone what He had done for them, they did it anyway. Considering how He had impacted them, how could anyone blame them if they did?

3. **The testimony of excited witnesses.**

Satisfied customers are like a light that recommends. However, an excited witness is a blaze that spreads like a wildfire. Such was the case with the Samaritan woman who Jesus met at the well. After talking with Jesus for merely a few minutes, she was so excited that she left her water pot at the well and ran into the city crying, "Come see a man ..." As a result, an entire town came out to get to know Jesus for themselves.

4. **The curiosity generated by His critics.**

Jesus had more than His fair share of criticism. However, in some cases that criticism only served to pique more curiosity about Him and therefore increased the number of people who desired to see Him. Zacchaeus climbed a tree to see Him. Nicodemus sneaked to Him by night. Thus, both positive and negative press made Him famous and drew crowds to Him.

5. **Giving a targeted assignment.**

Several people left Jesus with a testimony, but only rarely did Jesus command and commission them to do so. The man who had been a demoniac when he first met Jesus wanted to follow Jesus after his healing (Mark 5:18–20). Instead Jesus commanded him to go home to his friends and tell them what the Lord had done for him. In other words, the Lord gave him a targeted market that he was to cover as an ambassador for Him.

6. Dispatching disciples to spread the word about Him.

What Luke 10 describes seems almost like the advance team of a rock star about to go on tour. Here, Jesus sent out seventy of His disciples to visit towns He planned to enter. Their task was to prepare the way for Him and publicize His coming. Thus, by the time He arrived, people would already know who He was and be eager to receive what He had to offer.

If these worked for Jesus in the first century, they will still work for us in the twenty-first century. We can add our technology to His techniques and have an even greater numerical return than He did when we learn to: spotlight examples of changed lives; produce satisfied customers; give the microphone to excited witnesses; capitalize on negative criticism; target most receptive audiences; and use trained and committed disciples to spread the ministry throughout the community and the world.

Empty Plans

Plans draw people. Plans inspire people. Plans motivate people. Plans energize people. Plans galvanize people. That is why architects create color renderings. That is why restaurants place "Coming Soon" signs on vacant land. That is why a pastor or church cannot afford to give up on empty seats because plans fill empty seats with people.

Without a plan empty seats remain an ever-present sign of failure. With a plan, those same empty seats can be seen as an opportunity. (At least you have the empty seats and space to grow!)

For several pages, we have been identifying several factors that lead to empty seats. We have seen that empty preachers, empty preaching, empty people, empty praise, an empty place, an empty plate, and empty promotion are all contributing factors.

Now, in the end, if we read and agree even to some extent with the validity of these observations and leave this work without a plan, then the whole exercise will have been for naught.

Thus, the next step is for me to ask you, "Based on this book and what has been revealed to you in the process of reading it, are you going to be satisfied with the status quo, or are you going to attempt to fill those empty seats? If so, what is your plan?"

What is your plan to do the following?

1. Revisit, review, and recast the vision.

Chances are, you began your ministry with a vision, and that vision did not include empty seats. You saw a church full of passion and people. You envisioned a place alive with worship and enthusiastic about growing. You spoke of a congregation that was like a complete community.

What ever happened to that vision? Is it on a piece of paper in the file cabinet? Is the picture of it drawn on a poster board somewhere in your garage? Where is that vision? When was the last time you saw it? When was the last time you spoke about it? What is your plan to remember it, review it, revisit it, and even revise it?

2. Remove the barriers.

You may not have even needed this book to tell you why you have so many empty seats. You already know. What you haven't done is to make a plan to systematically remove the barriers that prevent your empty seats from being filled.

Deep down inside you know what needs to be done, but you fear that taking steps to remove these barriers might create even more empty seats, including yours! We are not just talking about removing the steps to make the building more accessible. We might be talking about removing some people as well to make the church more viable. If it must be done, what's your plan?

3. **Recruit a team.**

You cannot do what must be done to fill the empty seats in your church alone. What is your plan to recruit the help you will need to do it? Who will you ask? When will you ask? How many will you ask? What will you ask? How long will you plan? What is your plan to call together a core group that shares your heart, your vision, and your fire? They are already there in the church waiting to be asked to participate in the planning and the process of its implementation.

4. **Raise the resources.**

Even with the right team, you are still going to need resources to bring your plans off of the drawing board. What is your plan? What is your plan to raise money? What is your plan to reallocate money? What is your plan to challenge your church to a higher level of giving? What is your plan to partner with other agencies, businesses, and institutions?

5. Refill the seats.

The seats are empty because they were put there in the hope that one day they would be filled or they were once filled and for some reason became empty. Either way, whether they are being filled for the first time or refilled like old times, what is your plan?

You may want to adopt the plan of the householder in the parable of Jesus who sponsored a banquet and couldn't get many to come to it.

> Then He said to him, "A certain man gave a great supper and invited many, and sent his servant at supper time to say to those who were invited, 'Come, for all things are now ready.' But they all with one accord began to make excuses. The first said to him, 'I have bought a piece of ground, and I must go and see it. I ask you to have me excused.' And another said, 'I have bought five yoke of oxen, and I am going to test them. I ask you to have me excused.' Still another said, 'I have married a wife, and therefore I cannot come.' So that servant came and reported these things to his master. Then the master of the house, being angry, said to his servant, 'Go out quickly into the streets and lanes of the city, and bring in here the poor and the maimed and the lame and the blind.'

And the servant said, 'Master, it is done as you commanded, and still there is room.' Then the master said to the servant, 'Go out into the highways and hedges, and compel them to come in, that my house may be filled. For I say to you that none of those men who were invited shall taste my supper.'" (Luke 14:16–24)

In other words, "Go get 'em!"

Part II

More than One Hundred Steps to Fill God's House with People, Power, and Praise

The nine factors I have identified as contributing to empty seats in the church have been offered as a general description of the culprits. What follows is a proscriptive list of more than one hundred steps that you and your church can take to reduce the number of your empty seats.

Understand that these are steps. While any one of these could literally change your life and ministry, they are being suggested as incremental actions you can take in combination with others to increase your attendance on Sundays and the maturity of your membership.

You may already be doing some of what is being suggested. Other steps may not only be unthinkable but impossible for you. The items on this list are in random order, with no implication that any one is more or less important than another.

The list has simply been designed to be suggestive and not all-inclusive. When you hear good preaching, it makes you want to preach. When you read this list, I hope it generates even further steps in you. You are by no means limited to or bound by these recommendations. My prayer is that the Holy Ghost will put flesh on these bones and continue to give you greater revelation until your ministry rises in the valley as a mighty army.

The Preacher

1. **Face your empty seats, and own your part of the responsibility for their existence.** Even though it may not all be your fault, much of it is still your responsibility. Until you own them, you will not be able to fill them.
2. **Make your empty seats a matter of regular prayer in which you talk to and listen to God about them.** Let God know that they trouble you, and listen to God's direction on how to fill them.
3. **Immediately follow the Holy Spirit's promptings.** Knowing when to do is often as important, if not more important, than knowing what to do. Timing truly can be everything.
4. **Connect with a coach who has already done or is doing what God has placed in your heart to do.** Have your church consider any costs for this coaching as continuing education and put it in the budget, if necessary. It will benefit them as much as it will benefit you.
5. **See your empty seats as both a symptom of deficiency and a significant opportunity.** This is true especially if you are in the beginning stages of your ministry or the

beginning steps of rebooting your ministry. Your empty seats should not really judge you because you are at a stage where empty seats should be expected. Praise the Lord, you have space to grow.

6. **Know yourself and your gifts.** Surround yourself with trustworthy people who have complementary gifts and who are committed to your vision. In order to draw others to your church who are not exactly like you, you will need members and leaders who are like the people you want to reach who are not like you!

7. **Ask God to give you a heart to fill His kingdom with saved and sanctified souls—not simply to fill the empty seats in your sanctuary.** You cannot pull the wool over God's eyes. He knows your motives for filling the church. Don't expect Him to fill your church for you. His aim is to fill His kingdom for Him!

8. **Saturate yourself with books, tapes, videos, and other resources produced by successful pastors and churches.** Don't be a copycat or a poly parrot. Take what they have to offer and adapt it to your situation. Receive whatever you peruse the same way you eat fish: "Eat the meat and spit out the bones."

9. **Preach with your eyes closed.** This is not a form of denial. It is a technique to enable you to envision what will be while it is not. Periodic closed eyes brought me through many summer months during the early years of our church as we worshiped in a rented school. I closed my eyes and

preached like that auditorium was full. I envisioned it being full, and soon it was.

10. **Take some time off for your vocation that is not seen as a vacation.** Whether you call it a retreat or an advance, spend some time alone with God. He is waiting for you and eager to tell you what to do.

11. **Address the white elephants in the room.** Do not ignore undercurrents among the congregation or clouds that overcast your congregation in the eyes of the community. No matter what steps you take, they will be negated and overwhelmed if you do not deal with these real barriers affecting your growth. Such things as the church's reputation, open conflict within the church, or integrity issues in the pulpit will give present members and potential guests an excuse not to attend. Therefore, you will have to change the public perception of the church and resolve the internal issues even before you will be given consideration for membership.

12. **Be courageous.** Often the problem is not that we lack creativity or consciousness. What we lack is courage. We know what do. However, we are also quite aware that it will not be easy and perhaps even painful. Still, hear and receive what God told Joshua after the death of Moses and before they possessed the Promised Land.

> No man shall be able to stand before you all
> the days of your life; as I was with Moses, so
> I will be with you. I will not leave you nor

forsake you. Be strong and of good courage, for to this people you shall divide as an inheritance the land which I swore to their fathers to give them. Only be strong and very courageous, that you may observe to do according to all the law which Moses My servant commanded you; do not turn from it to the right hand or to the left, that you may prosper wherever you go. This Book of the Law shall not depart from your mouth, but you shall meditate in it day and night, that you may observe to do according to all that is written in it. For then you will make your way prosperous, and then you will have good success. Have I not commanded you? Be strong and of good courage; do not be afraid, nor be dismayed, for the Lord your God is with you wherever you go. (Joshua 1:5–9)

The Preaching

13. **Change your focus from what you would like to preach to what those in front of you need to hear.** No one is really interested in how many German theologians you can quote or even how much Hebrew and Greek you have mastered. The ones who sit before you each week come with the same request that the Greeks made of Philip in John 12:21: "Sir, we wish to see Jesus."
14. **Preach to the people who are in the seats vs. focusing on the empty seats.** Yes, this whole book is about how to fill the empty seats. However, if you focus on the empty seats and fail to minister to the ones who are there filling some seats, you will end up losing them too. Fill the people who fill the seats. Then the full people will spread the word and, in turn, fill the empty seats with their family and friends. (By the way, don't forget to count the children and youth who may be in the building but not in the main sanctuary when you preach. They are vital to your church growth and future.)
15. **Preach series.** One thing that keeps people coming is a series over several weeks on a topic addressing a felt need.

Most of these topics cannot be covered in one sermon anyway. A series on marriage, parenting, prosperity, faith, tithing, witnessing, stress, worship, praise, healing, and more can not only bless your church members but also keep them coming.

16. **Connect your preaching to your Bible study teaching.** In order to decrease the number of empty seats in both your Sunday worship time and your Bible study time, link the two by dealing with the same subject at both. The teaching's objective is to give followers a godly foundation and sound biblical information. The sermon aims at persuading and prompting those same individuals into action. Over time, you can build a mature congregation that not only acts godly but also knows why.

17. **Stick to the Bible.** You would think that this point should not even have to be added. Nevertheless, it has been added because empty seats might lead one to a sense of desperation. That desperation could lead to unscrupulous and questionable methods to fill the seats.

If you raffled off a Mercedes every week, you would fill your seats. But how many Mercedes can you buy and give away? Besides that, you would be creating a crowd that just came for the car! You want the church to be filled with those who are there for Christ. That's why everything you do should pass the: "Is it biblical?" test.

18. **Invite trusted guest preachers who are specialists as preachers and/or teachers in the areas in which you desire your church to grow (e.g., stewardship, soul winning, mission).** They can help to lay the foundation for the growth and development of your church. You don't have to do it all yourself. In fact, you can't do it all yourself. After the specialists have come, be prepared to follow up on what they shared. The benefits of their preaching and teaching will fizzle out without your conscious follow up.

19. **Back up the preaching with programs and/or practical action steps people can take in response to the preaching.** Before you launch a program or ministry, preach about the value of it or the biblical mandate to do it. This way, you preach about an action and then give those who will hear a viable option to put it into action.

A great sermon becomes a lasting sermon when it is connected to a concrete ministry that keeps it alive. Be careful, though, not to preach the sermon and get people fired up if you are not ready to release them to the ministry. Otherwise you will lose the momentum the message created.

The People

20. **Teach your people to invite family and friends.** Many church members are afraid to evangelize. They are terrified at the thought of leading anyone to Christ, not to mention a total stranger. Inviting family and friends to worship is much easier for your members and much less threatening to their family and friends. Even so, your members must be encouraged and taught to invite guests to your church in a loving and nonjudgmental way.
21. **Train a core group to evangelize.** Not everyone in your church has the gift of evangelism, but some do. Call together a core group of those with such a gift and train them to do evangelism in your community, with family and friends of your members and among the guests who visit your church. The hottest prospects to evangelize are those who have come to your church and actually indicate that they would like to accept Christ and/or join your church. You may have a whole evangelism field in the response cards of your visitors. Go figure!
22. **Have a group in your church to pray for God to send the souls to fill the seats.** Pray for and anoint the seats as

if they were people. Pray that the Lord of the harvest will send laborers into the harvest. When you have others pray for the empty seats, now these seats are not just on your mind but on the minds of the rest of the church as well.

23. **Challenge the people to see the seats as souls and then to fill the seats accordingly.** If you promote filling the seats just for the sake of having a full house, it may come off as self-serving. However, if you teach your church to see each seat as a soul, then they are not just filling the sanctuary; they are filling heaven. It has an even greater impact if they can envision someone they love sitting in that seat and on their way to heaven.

24. **Have a revival and invite a preacher with an evangelistic heart and gift.** Technically, a revival is to rekindle the fire for those who already know the Lord. But practically, it can be one of the best tools to introduce the unsaved to the gospel and the unchurched to your ministry.

Let me reiterate, make sure that the revivalist has a heart for souls and a gift of evangelism. Also, intentionally take steps to get as many unsaved and unchurched people as possible in attendance. If you don't, you may get a week of preaching to the choir and no one to fill the empty seats.

25. **Account for all your people.** Sometimes, you already have enough members to fill the seats. Don't wait until you are getting ready to have a hot church meeting to clean up your church roster. Clean it, clear it, and then

follow up on your own members. Find out where they are and why they don't come. You would be surprised at how much of a difference a single phone call from the church will make.

26. **Make a fuss over guests.** First of all, do not refer to nonmembers as visitors. A visitor is someone who comes to your house uninvited and often unwelcomed. Guests, on the other hand, are invited, expected, and hosted with kindness and love. Then, after you change how you look at them, make a big deal over them. Sincerely welcome them. Acknowledge them. Give information to them. Give gifts to them. Follow up on them. Everyone loves a little extra attention.

27. **Train your greeters, guest services, and ushers ministries.** In order to make the experience of coming to your church pleasant, you will want to create various ministries whose task it is to make sure that happens. Pleasant and smiling greeters at the doors are the first friendly faces guests meet. Between the front doors and the sanctuary doors should be the guest services ministry. Their job is to identify and register the guests so they can be better recognized and tracked. Courteous and Christian ushers are critical in getting the guests to their seats as soon as possible, respecting both the worship and the guests. It takes a team to provide this experience. When it is done properly, it is so seamless that the guests feel it, but may not even notice the thought, practice, and prayer you put into it.

28. **Follow up on guests in a systematic but nonaggressive manner.** Those who have been to your church have already filled an empty seat at least once. Therefore, they know how it feels. While that feeling (which we assume will be a positive one) is still fresh, call them, write them, or by some means contact them after their visit to thank them and invite them to come again. This process not only lets the guests know you appreciate them, but their comments will also let you know how your church is doing from their perspective.

29. **Administer a spiritual gifts survey to current members and all new members.** This is not a test. It is a tool that includes a series of questions that will allow those who take it to learn the types of spiritual gifts they have. What you then do is match their gifts with ministries in your church that require those gifts. You have people sitting inactive because they are not aware of their spiritual gifts or where to use them. This survey empowers them and stirs them into service. Begin with yourself and your leaders. Then offer it to all of your members and require it of all of your new members. You can find these online and may even be able to incorporate one on your church website.

30. **Where you can't replace leaders who block the advancement of the church, create new ministries and add new leaders.** If you are in an established church, it may be extremely difficult, if not impossible, to move old, uninspired leadership. Doing so could cost peace in

the church or even your job. Instead of firing old people, add new people! Create new ministries and new leaders without the baggage of the previous ones, and let the church roll on!

The Place

31. **Remove extra seats, and use the remaining space creatively.** Instead of trying to fill the empty seats, remove them. You don't need them right now anyway. So if it is not totally impractical, move them out of sight. Then use the extra space as flexible space for classes, information tables, members' services, or something along these lines. You may be able to put a partition in the sanctuary to make it seem smaller. But don't do anything permanent because one day you expect to bring those seats back!
32. **Host events that will fill the church. (e.g., concerts, community events, association or convention meetings).** This gives your people a concrete picture of what the church would look like full.

When I became the pastor of my first church in Providence, Rhode Island, I found a huge church with a sanctuary that was designed to seat one thousand but might have had one hundred and fifty to two hundred attendees on a good Sunday. I remember one elderly deaconess saying to me upon my arrival that all she wanted was to see that church full one time before she died.

A few weeks later, at my installation, with seven busloads of my family and friends from my hometown in Baltimore, Maryland, and two busloads from Cambridge, Massachusetts, where I had been going to school and worshiping, the church was soon full. This deaconess saw the church full before she died and lived long enough to see it full on a regular basis.

33. **Add on to your church.** It does not seem to make sense to add anything when you have empty seats. Well, it does if you add space to provide ministries and services that will draw people to your church. This includes adding a nursery, gymnasium, family life center, community center, banquet hall, classroom space, day care center, or even Christian school. What you add may not immediately get people into the sanctuary, but it does get them in the door.
34. **Merge with another congregation.** I know that this is unthinkable, but it may be the only thing practical and reasonable. Your building may be too big for your ministry. However, when merged with another, the facility may be perfect. Of course, this is tricky because fitting in the same building is one thing. Fitting together in ministry under a unified leadership is entirely another.
35. **Merge two services into one.** You may have empty seats because you have two or more services each Sunday morning. If you only had one service, your sanctuary might be packed.

Be careful, though, before you move to one service. There is a crowd that will only come early and a crowd that will only come late. If you move the service to sometime in the middle, you may end up losing worshipers on both ends and still have empty seats. It is better to minister to more people at different times with empty seats than to reach a packed house with less people all at once.

36. **Make your church look more like a mall than a museum.** Your church should not be a shopping mall, but it could offer a variety of ministries in a variety of spaces like a mall offers goods for sale. Today's population is quite comfortable in spending hours upon hours in a mall. It is hard to get this contemporary crowd to feel comfortable in a building that looks like a dark dungeon with pictures of dead people staring at them as they walk through its narrow halls. It is possible to have a church that feels like a mall and at the same time has an air of holiness.

37. **Keep up the outside of your church.** Remember: the outside of your church is your physical calling card. The public sees it and makes a judgment about you before they even meet you or know your name. Therefore, keep up the outside of your church. You may be able to recruit a team of people to do this as volunteers if you cannot afford to hire someone to do it.

38. **Get a good PA system so people can hear.** If you prepare a good sermon, you want somebody to hear it. If the choir has practiced all week and is on fire (and hopefully

also on key), they too want to be heard. An investment in a good PA system with competent people to run it is worth its weight in gold.

39. **Partner with or rent other facilities like the YMCA or a nearby school to do your ministry there, if you don't have the space.** You could have a large sanctuary and that's all. So, expand your ministry by partnering with other facilities. You may not have a gym, but the YMCA does. Use their facility to do your sports ministry. You may not have classrooms, but the school has plenty that are not being used on Sunday. This way you can build your ministry without having to immediately build new buildings.

40. **Use small groups as a way of growing your church and geographically spreading your ministry impact without adding space to your church.** You may not have the one room full at one time, but you could reach the same amount of people in different places at different times. Small groups are really as old as the early church that had no church building at all. They met from house to house. Small groups allow your church to grow exponentially without you having to add classroom and meeting space.

41. **Create parking.** You have space to put the people, but where will the people put their cars if they come? There are countless successful churches in major metropolitan areas that have virtually no parking. They are ministry miracles and a nuisance to their neighbors. Ample parking and even excess parking removes one significant barrier to a person

who would like to worship at your church. If you can't add parking space near the church, buy or lease land down the street and run a shuttle from there to your church.

42. **See your building as a community center and not only as a worship center.** Churches with empty seats tend to also have empty rooms. That is to say, the sanctuary is not the only space that is empty, and Sunday is not the only time the church is empty. Thousands of square feet are used for only a few hours on Sunday and Bible study on Wednesday. When the church building is seen as a community center, then activities other than worship can take place there and people other than members can be served there.

43. **Move.** If you think moving old leadership is cause for trouble, try moving the whole church. You are just asking for it! But moving is often a very good solution if you can bring your congregation along with the idea. Sometimes your building and its location is your worst enemy. No amount of renovation will make it fit the vision God has given to you. If you can't do it there, you may have to move.

The Praise

44. **Distinguish between devotions and praise.** For many years, African American churches have had a period of Scripture, prayer, and singing before worship that they call "devotions." Typically, a few deacons (many of whom do not sing well) stand before the few on-time worshipers and sing "down home songs" or call out songs by number from a hymnbook. This is not what I mean by praise and worship. Most of these songs focus on the person singing and not God. They talk about my trouble, my sickness, my need, etc., instead of the goodness and greatness of God. Praise of God should be about God!
45. **Give prime time to praise.** Actually, singing songs of praise to God before the worship is what many churches do now. Ironically, they have essentially replaced the devotions, and the praise period has literally become the prelude. This is a step in the right direction; however, it still relegates praise to being a warm up to the real worship. You will be surprised how much power and spirit you can bring to your worship experience by incorporating praise and worship songs in prime time throughout the worship.

This way, no matter when people arrive during the service, they won't miss it.

46. **Organize a praise team.** Just as a few deacons who do not sing well are usually ineffective leading devotions, so will be a few committed saints who may even know how to sing, but do not have a heart or passion for praise and worship. Your praise team or praise leader should know how to praise the Lord and love to praise the Lord. If you don't have a praise team, start with a "praise person." Then give your praise leaders the time and freedom to lead the congregation in praise until the Holy Spirit comes.

47. **Fill the atmosphere with praise before you fill the seats with people.** When your seats are empty, your first move should be to fill the hearts of the ones who are there with prayer and the atmosphere with praise. Just a few people can praise the Lord in such a powerful way that it will attract the ones you need to fill your empty seats. There may be dozens of reasons why you can't fill your seats with people. However, there is no excuse for not filling the air in the sanctuary with praise.

48. **Use hymns that focus on Him.** There is nothing wrong with hymns. They have been the backbone of our worship for centuries. Many of them have gotten us through tough times when we couldn't recall a Scripture. What is being emphasized here is that the presence of the Lord comes more quickly when even the hymns we sing are about Him. If you use hymnbooks, please take the time to select

and sing songs about God. There are dozens of hymns that praise, worship, and exalt the Lord. Find them and sing them to the glory of God.

49. **Add instruments.** I remember how much of a fight it was in one of the churches I pastored when we introduced drums into the worship. It was a big deal. Eventually they were accepted, and so were the synthesizer, bass guitar, and more. In my current church, we have a small orchestra. Christians have been led to believe that instruments in the church are worldly and that such belongs to the Devil.

Not only is this not correct, it is not biblical. Psalm 150 is perfect proof of this:

> Praise the Lord! Praise God in His sanctuary; Praise Him in His mighty firmament! Praise Him for His mighty acts; Praise Him according to His excellent greatness! Praise Him with the sound of the trumpet; Praise Him with the lute and harp! Praise Him with the timbrel and dance; Praise Him with stringed instruments and flutes! Praise Him with loud cymbals; Praise Him with clashing cymbals! Let everything that has breath praise the Lord. Praise the Lord!

50. **Either incorporate a variety of music in your single worship or offer other worship experiences with a variety of different types of music.** Worship is like food.

Everybody has to eat, but everybody does not like Italian! If completely changing over to more praise and worship songs is too much of a challenge, consider offering separate worships with an emphasis on different types of music. This way, you can keep the ones who love the hymns and also the ones who prefer more praise and worship songs. Then sprinkle a little of each in both.

51. **Use music tracks to add a professional and big sound.** There is a church in our city that has no choir and no musicians. No problem. Instead, believe it or not, they have a DJ! I know it sounds crazy, but they have a small praise team that stands before the church and leads them in singing top-forty gospels songs from CDs of the original artists. They are able to pull it off in such a way that it does not sound canned. It actually sounds great!

You may not want to go all the way as they do. However, there are many music tracks you can purchase to use as the instrumentation for your praise and worship. It will instantly give a big and professional sound to your worship.

52. **Use large video screens or TV monitors to free the people's hands.** The mere mechanics of hymnbooks make it more difficult to focus on God. That is because reading the words and your congregation burying their heads in the books do not allow those who are singing to do so freely. That's why you may have heard it said that the

church doesn't really start to sing until they put down the hymnbooks.

It is not the hymn or the book. It is the attention to the book that makes it hard to give total attention to God. Even though your parishioners will still be reading when they look at a large video screen, they can do it hands free! Those free hands can now clap and be lifted in praise.

53. **Incorporate gospel arts in worship**. Psalm 150 also indicates that we can worship God with more than singing. We can also do it with instruments and dance. These days, more and more churches are using gospel arts to worship the Lord. Dance, mime, spoken word, rapping, puppets, signing, bell choir, flag, and step are examples of this. If you do not yet have a ministry in your church that can minister in this way, consider inviting guest artists to come. Allowing your church to see these means of worshiping in their space may inspire them to start their own ministry. Don't limit your worship to singing. God is much bigger than that.

54. **Remove the fluff and unnecessary line items from worship.** As you review your order of worship, identify portions of worship that have nothing to do with worship and then cut them out. Worship can have everlasting effects without lasting forever.

55. **Do a preaching and/or teaching series on praise and worship.** Although we all were created to praise and

worship God, praise and worship are not natural to all of us. Therefore, praise and worship must be taught like everything else. Consider preaching and teaching on the importance of praise, postures of praise, impact of praise, power of praise, and products of praise.

The Plate

56. **Make it easy for your members and guests to give.** Talk with your bank on how to set up an account where your members can give using their debit or credit cards. You can have a space for their information on your regular church envelope, or create separate slips for it.
57. **Create prepaid envelopes which members can use to mail their offerings to you at no cost to the giver.** This way the US Post Office's letter carriers become your ushers and take up the collection for you from anywhere in the country.
58. **You can also install a machine that allows members to swipe their debit/credit cards or acquire such a machine for your own finance team to swipe the cards.** There are companies that can install a kiosk in your church lobby to allow people to give anytime they are in the building. I am not personally a fan of ATMs in the church, although some have used these to facilitate giving. The main idea is the easier it is to give, the more likely people will be to give.

59. **Use PayPal or some related service to enable your members and friends to donate online at your website.**
60. **Have a stewardship revival where total stewardship is promoted, including, but not limited to, tithing.** Instead of wining souls, your aim during this revival will be to win better stewards. Make sure you ask for commitments in the same way that you invite converts to Christ. From this revival you hope to win stewardship converts.

The Programs

61. **Make disciples.** Please highlight and place flashing red lights on this point. You are wasting your time if all you do is put butts in the seats. They will never return on a regular basis unless you have programs in place to help these butts develop and grow into mature believers who no longer have to be chased and begged to come to church. Have classes for new members that orient them to the church and Christianity. Have basic discipleship classes that expose them to basic Christian beliefs and practices. Teach them how to study the Bible, how to pray, how to give, how to evangelize and more. This whole book is about filling the empty seats, but the next step (which could be the subject of another book) is how to fill and disciple the new people who now fill your empty seats. By visiting your Christian bookstore or searching "discipleship resources" online, you can get an excellent start to finding resources to help you create an effective discipleship program for your church.
62. **Do outreach that invites community people in.** Not everyone is interested in or ready to worship at your church. Still, you can offer them a reason to come to your

church by creating outreach programs that are based in your church. Consider: an after-school program, day care center, food pantry, free meal, clothing give away, AA meetings, grief recovery programs, or Financial Peace University workshop.

63. **Do outreach that sends your members out into the community.** In other words, minister inside out. The energy of the typical church is directed outside in. Its efforts are primarily based on trying to get people to come into the church. However, making a directional shift where the church invests more energy into getting the church members and ministry out into the community is bound to result in getting the community to then come into the church.

64. **Minister in places that have a built-in full house.** Everyone does not have empty seats. There are packed places that would welcome you with open arms. Schools, colleges, nursing homes, prisons, shelters, and more offer you a chance to minister with no empty seats. Again, the focus is the impact of your ministry, not how much of it takes place on Sunday in your sanctuary.

65. **Institute specialized ministries.** Separate ministries for men, women, children, youth, families, singles, parents, couples, and more will enable your church to minister to your own members in a more targeted manner. It also offers a place for their friends to come and participate in the church without having to be members.

Preaching to Empty Seats

66. **Model Jesus in your practices.** According to Matthew 9:35, Jesus had a varied but simple ministry. Everything He did fell under one of the following categories: preaching, teaching, or healing. He reached the whole world with this model. You can too.

67. **Do fun stuff with fellowship as its goal.** Never underestimate the value of good, clean Christian fellowship. Where can it be found? The Adversary has thousands of options for fun that are not all clean or Christian. Why not offer opportunities for people to have fun together?

You don't have to do Bible study every time you gather. Try a bowling league, movie night, church cookout, Christmas party, couples' night out, bus trip, or even a day at an amusement park. Church is not just to get to know God better. It is also for the saints to get to know each other better.

68. **Feed the people.** Free food always draws a crowd. Just be ready to offer solid spiritual food after they eat. A weekly or monthly meal for the community will give you a chance to feed people in more ways than one.

69. **Church school doesn't have to be on Sunday, but it does give your people an opportunity to grow.** The late Dr. Harold A. Carter Sr. of the New Shiloh Baptist Church in Baltimore, Maryland, pioneered the idea of church school on Saturday. By means of this, he built a phenomenal ministry. Saturday school gave more time for teaching and the addition of other creative teaching techniques. You may

not want to do your "Sunday" school on Saturday, but remember it doesn't have to be on Sunday. Turn your Bible study into "Sunday" school or at least an extension of it with a variety of graded classes and interests groups.

70. **Offer an online Bible study.** While we were building our new church, we did not have a place to hold Bible study during the week. The Lord gave me the idea to have the Bible study on the telephone. I called it Bible Study for Busy People. Each week, I recorded a five- to ten-minute Bible study on the telephone. People would call a toll free number 24–7 to listen to the study, follow along in a workbook I had written, answer questions, and be given homework. In total, I had twice as many attendees on the phone than I ever had at the traditional Bible study.

Today, with the advent of the Internet, it is much easier to do Bible study online. Everyone can't make it to Bible study at 7:00 p.m. on Wednesday. If you record it and make it available, they can do Bible study at 3:00 a.m. on Thursday if they choose! We stream our Bible study live online and then record it so those who miss it live can watch it at their convenience 24–7.

71. **Partner with government agencies and other community organizations to offer ministry.** You may not have the manpower to offer major ministry, but you do have the space. There are agencies in your community that have the manpower but not the space. Team up with them and bless the community.

Every month our church is able to distribute twenty thousand pounds of fresh fruits and vegetables free to the community. We are only able to do this because we became a distribution site for the local food bank. Each month we feed more than five hundred families. That's five hundred families who come through our doors who otherwise would never enter. We could never do this alone. But we can by partnering.

72. **Invest in a van and bring the people in.** This is by no means new. It is a great challenge with the high cost of fuel these days. Nevertheless, your bus may be your greatest evangelistic asset. One stop at a nursing home, shelter, or housing development can fill your bus and a bunch of empty seats.

73. **You can have a full ministry with empty seats because your ministry is larger than your attendance and your membership.** This point is just to call to your attention something that you may have overlooked. Your ministry is always larger than your attendance. For example, you may have a woman who belongs to your church whose husband and children do not. If her husband goes to the hospital and you visit him, you are expanding your ministry but not necessarily filling an empty seat. Your perception of your success changes radically when you begin to consider how many you minister to instead of how many you physically preach to.

74. **Make your church available for community groups and agencies whose goals are compatible with yours.**

Earlier, we mentioned partnering with community groups to offer programs. Here, we are suggesting that you offer your empty space to such groups to actually house their programs inside of your church. They would be run by them and simply be housed by you. Whether you do it free or for a fee, many of them have people and funds but no space. You have no people and no funds but plenty of space, so it could be a perfect match.

The Promotion

75. **A changed life is the best advertisement.** Highlight and spotlight the testimonies and stories of those whose lives have been changed for the better because of your ministry.
76. **Excited members are most effective.** Encourage your members to talk about your church and ministry. Give them tools to spread the word about your church and the Lord. They can and will travel places you never will.
77. **Develop a motto or mission statement that shares your vision.** Many churches have mottos that say nothing about what the church is about. Your motto or slogan should be so simple, succinct, and provocative that it creates interest in the minds of those who read it.
78. **Use radio and television.** Through a radio or television broadcast, you can reach more people than you could ever seat in your sanctuary. However, a thirty- or sixty-minute broadcast in some cities would cost more than the church's monthly mortgage. Instead consider thirty- or sixty-second spots consisting of a brief message and advertisement of your church to run throughout the week. Not only is this

cheaper, but you will also have a chance to reach more people more often.

79. **Visibility at community festivals, fairs, etc.** Every city has festivals where the whole community gathers to celebrate various occasions. Get a booth like everyone else and promote your Lord and your ministry. If you don't get a booth, hand out free bottles of water, tracts, or flyers to share your ministry with the community. Don't wait for them to come to you. You go to them.

80. **Specialize in special days to celebrate people.** Special days are not only fun, but through them you can honor and celebrate people. Since everyone likes a little celebration, they will show up and bring their friends to see them honored. Here is a list of some of the special days we observe in addition to regular holidays: monthly birthdays, Women's Day, Men's Day, Children's Day, Youth and Young Adult Day, pastor's anniversary, First Lady Sunday, Friend Day, Seniors' and Grandparents' Day, Teacher Appreciation Day, Sickle Cell Sabbath, Veterans Day, Graduates Sunday, and Pink Sunday for cancer awareness. Use your imagination. Celebrate everybody and everything all the time.

81. **Send out press releases.** There are two ways to get in the newspaper. The first is to write a press release and tell them what you are doing. The second way is to do something newsworthy and they will come and ask you what you are doing. Either way, a newspaper that has a circulation in the tens of thousands can reach more people than you will ever seat or see at one time. All of this at no cost to you.

82. **Advertise on your local free cable TV community station.** Every city has a local free public cable channel. This station exists to serve the community. Some cities allow religious programming. In this instance, you could produce a television show and have it aired for free on cable to your whole community. At a minimum, you can have announcements about your church activities aired each week for free. Call your cable company and ask how you can get started.

83. **Special days to invite guests.** Above, we spoke of special days to recognize and honor people. This series of special days is to give your members a reason to invite their family and friends to come to church. Dr. Elmer Towns' Friend Day and F.R.A.N.gelism (Friends, Relatives, Associates, and Neighbors) have been used for decades to pack churches with guests. More recently, National Back to Church Sunday on the third Sunday in September has also been an effective vehicle to fill the house of God.

84. **Create a media ministry.** High on the list of promotion must be the establishment and development of a media ministry. This ministry not only provides the sound for worship, but tapes, CDs, videos, DVDs, Internet, video announcements, newsletters, websites, Internet TV channels, and more. There is no better way to project your ministry than with a media ministry that gets what you do beyond your walls.

85. **Put a sign outside the church.** You might think this is too obvious to mention. Still, many church signs are

too small to see. The words are too small to read. The information on them is irrelevant to those who pass by. It does not have to be electronic or fancy. However, you only have about seven seconds for passengers in cars to read your sign. In that time period, you not only communicate information to them, but the condition of the sign itself communicates how much you care about your ministry. When done right, those who regularly pass by your church will look forward to the inspirational messages that you post. Now your sign has become a ministry.

86. **Street ministry.** Ironically, while you are trying to get more people into the empty seats, you may have members who are really more comfortable doing ministry outside of the church. They are not ashamed, embarrassed, or afraid to witness, pray for, or serve total strangers on the street. Go ahead and release them to do it!

87. **Go all out on Christmas, Mother's Day, and Easter.** These are the three times when you may expect more people to think about coming to church. Instead of having an attitude because of the CMEs (people who only come to church on Christmas, Mother's Day, and Easter), anticipate their coming and make a big deal out of it and them. Have special music and special presentations. Give out small gifts like candy for the children. If you know they are going to come, don't miss this golden opportunity.

88. **Arm your people with simple tools to do outreach and evangelism.** To make it easy to get the word out about your church, create postcards, brochures, business

cards, CDs, and DVDs your members can carry all the time and hand out freely. All of these have an indefinite shelf life that means that even a year later, it may prompt someone to try your church.

89. **Have members pass out church info during Halloween trick or treat.** Our children's ministry creates little slips of paper that have positive affirmations for children and the name and address of our church. Our members hand them out along with candy on Halloween.

90. **Promotion within the church.** External promotion is important, but don't forget to promote your ministry within your walls. Use a newsletter on paper or online. Try bulletin boards and video slides, as well as video announcements during worship. Check out mass texting and e-mail. The idea is not to forget to communicate with the people who are already coming so as to maximize their participation.

91. **Build a website.** It is unthinkable that any church today exists without a website. Your website can become your virtual church. There, members and friends can do everything except touch you. They will be able to see, hear, feel, give, and respond. A website instantly takes your church global as you now have a worldwide presence on the worldwide web.

It is not as hard as you may think. Companies like Godaddy.com can reasonably provide you with an address, storage space, and a template for a website you can customize. There are even sites that will allow you to create a website for free. If you don't know how to do it, ask your teenage child or grandchild!

92. **Update your system of communication.** The US Post Office is going bankrupt for a reason. It is too slow, and it costs too much. By texting and e-mailing, you can instantly communicate with your membership for routine information or emergencies. There are many companies that offer this service for a small fee. Some church office software includes a feature that will let you do this through their system so you won't have to buy another program.

93. **Stream worship.** With a camcorder purchased from Best Buy or Wal-Mart, you can connect to the Internet and stream your worship live around the world. Your shut-in members and extended church family can keep connected with you from anywhere. The key is how many you touch, not necessarily how many you see.

94. **Use social media.** Consider Facebook, Twitter, Instagram, and YouTube. I am not a cheerleader for social media. However, I know its power and that there are millions who use it as their primary means of communicating. There are ways to keep it clean and block unwanted content, so you may want to hold your nose and take the plunge. There's a whole world out there. They are already talking. You may as well get them talking about Jesus and you.

95. **Create your own Internet channel on YouTube.** Along the same lines of streaming video, you can create your own YouTube channel and do your own video programming,

which reaches around the world for free. Go to YouTube.com and get started now. Then promote your channel to everyone you can think of.

96. **Capitalize on events like weddings, baby dedications, baptisms, first communions, "right hand of fellowship," and even funerals to expose new people to church.** These spiritual rites of passage draw guests to your church who may otherwise not come. Be prepared to tactfully and tastefully welcome them and give them information about your church, as well as an invitation to return.

97. **Get involved with your community by being represented at community meetings.** Every day you probably receive invitations in the mail to attend meetings that you cannot. Develop a team of ambassadors who will represent you and the church at these meetings. Now you won't have to go, but the community can tell you care because you are represented at the table. This is a great assignment for associate ministers.

98. **Post signs to direct people to your church.** If your church is out of the way, you may want to post some signs directing people to your church. God forbid even with GPS, the guests trying to reach you get lost and give up. Besides, the signs are great for advertisement 24–7 as well as directions.

The Plans

99. **Incorporate your spouse and family in your planning process.** Their perspective from a different gender and different generation can be challenging but invaluable. They can easily see opportunities you cannot. Give them a chance to plan and participate in the implementation and leadership.

100. **Embrace technology.** So many church functions can be carried out much more efficiently and effectively using technology. You can computerize membership and finances. You can keep track of your facility usage. You can communicate with your membership by texts and e-mail. The main idea is not to be afraid of technology. It can bless your ministry and make up for staff and volunteers you do not have. Here again, if you do not understand how to use this technology, there are many available services that will teach you and help you.

101. **Change the time of worship.** A half-hour change here or there, or adding another day, could make all the difference in the world. The Bible does not require that we worship at 11:00 a.m. Take a survey of your membership and ask them which times they prefer. It might be well worth it.

102. **Maintain a standard of excellence for all you do, even if it is on a small scale.** You don't have to be big to plan big or look big. When excellence is your standard, it is noticeable and attractive.

103. **Write the vision and make it plain.** Doing this will force you to clarify what your vision is and help you better communicate it to your people. There should be an overall vision with associated visions for each area of ministry. For the most part, church folk will cooperate if we properly communicate to them. We can't communicate a vision that we don't have.

104. **Conveniences are as important, if not more important, to some people.** Before they designate you as "my church," they will want to know what are you going to do for "my children," "my car," "my schedule," and "my challenges." Perks beyond the preaching and praise are really important. By offering these conveniences, you remove barriers and take away excuses for not attending.

105. **Prioritize your objectives based on how they impact people, not property.** The costs of the building can become so high that all of your resources are funneled toward paying for and maintaining it. Still, unless significant resources in time and money are directed to building and maintaining people, you may have a beautiful building with a bunch of empty seats. It takes people to pay for the building, and that takes prioritizing and meeting their needs, which brings them into the building.

A Parting Prayer

Dear Lord,

I worship You because of Your greatness. I praise You because of Your goodness. I love You because of Your forgiveness.

Thank You for the call You have placed on my life. Thank You for the words You have put in my mouth. Thank You for the work You have assigned to my hands. Thank You for the dreams You have laid on my heart.

Please fill me with Your power so that I might preach, teach, live, and serve with a contagious anointing that enables me to fill empty seats in the sanctuary and gives me the privilege of helping to fill empty seats in heaven. Amen.

Other books by Dr. C. Dexter Wise III

No Place for a Prophet: *An Unconventional Preacher Trapped in a Traditional Church*
Everything You Need to Know to Preach Like a Pro
Divine Babies: *How to Give Birth to the Blessing God has Conceived Inside of You*
Stand: *Seven Sermons for Saints in a Red Sea Situation*
The ABC's of Effective Parenting
Twenty-One Words to Get Your Child Twenty-One
Faith That Works
Too Much Drama
How to Build the World's Greatest Men's Ministry
How to Live Life on Purpose
How to Have Joy on the Job (Audio Book)

Contact Dr. Wise at:

Dr. C. Dexter Wise III
Wise Works, Inc.
P.O. Box 0771
Westerville, OH 43086
(614) 898-1997
www.wiseworksonline.com

Printed in the United States
By Bookmasters